# LETTERS FROM A LOST SOUL

Carlin W. Allen / Letters from a Lost Soul

# LETTERS FROM A LOST SOUL

Carlin W. Allen

## COPYRIGHT DISCLAIMER

All imagery and scenarios presented or described in this book are fictitious. Any similarity to actual persons, living or dead, is coincidental.

Copyright © 2024 Carlin W. Allen

All rights reserved. No part of this book may be reproduced or used in any manner without the prior written permission of the copyright owner, except for the use of brief quotations in a book review.

# AUTHOR'S OTHER BOOKS

## Humanity Poetry Collection Series

Hues of Humanity: A Poetry Collection

Threads of Bohemia: Another Poetry Collection

# TABLE OF CONTENTS

*LETTERS FROM A LOST SOUL* --------------------- **3**
    LOVE ---------------------------------------------------------- **11**
    LOSS ---------------------------------------------------------- **51**
    REBIRTH ---------------------------------------------------- **83**

Dedicated to those courageous enough to fight the darkness to find the path back to the light.

# LOVE

## *November 23: Letters*

I'm Saul. Hi. And hello.
Welcome to my written parlor.
I'm generally pretty mellow,
but friends said writing these letters
would help me feel some kind of better…

I don't know who you are just yet,
but I am sure we've met in dreams.
I'm hoping to get my feet wet,
that someone may follow downstream,
perhaps help me catch some moonbeams…

This is a tale of love and loss,
and the journey back to the light,
when it seemed there were only costs,
and nothing from those I loved right.
This is a tale… of my "good fight."

## *December 18: Unhappy Holidays*

Burning candles. Snow-capped trees.
Happy elves sing joyfully.
Dreidels spinning endlessly.
Alone again. No mystery…

Summer friends invite me out.
They keep calling, scream and shout.
Why'd I have to give up cloud?
Wish the world would leave me be…

I miss when times were simpler.
When all that mattered to me
were light shows, sick beats and P.L.U.R.
Not seeking what I can't see…

The more the morning suns rise,
so much colder I become.
For each heart, a thousand tries.
No good it does anyone…

Cap your candles. Burn your trees.
Spin dreidels away from me.
Please stop singing hopelessly.
Just go away. Leave me be…

## *December 26: My Life's Dream*

Another relationship come and gone,

as seasonal as the common cold.

What I'd give for love which endures.

A love that defies all odds,

flying high in the clouds

proclaiming itself

from mountaintops,

to world's end.

Sweetly.

Love.

Life's dream.

Eternal.

Faithful and pure.

Unconditional,

breaking every rule,

basking in its own glory,

echoing across time and space.

Warm, like the light of a newborn sun.

Persistently true. Beautifully free.

## *January 1: If Only*

It is Friday on a Thursday.
Don't know where I've seen you before.
I'm not quite sure what I would say,
but I'm dreaming you'd come my way.
We could get to know the dance floor…

Two drinks.
Four happy feet.
Eight beats and steps to stay in sync.
Sixteen different ways I can think
we can get close after we meet…

I'm so captivated by how
you move and speak so gracefully.
Starry eyes are moonlit windows
I cannot stop thinking about.
I love it when you smile at me…

Two hearts.
Four holding hands.

Eight reasons we can't stay apart.
Sixteen hours until we can start
loving one another firsthand.

## *January 29: In Love*

Yes, you said yes!
Of all the people,
you thought I was the best.
Underneath a steeple…
…it's a sign for the rest!

Shh! Play it cool.
It is like chess.
Stop acting like a fool.
Yes, *of course*, you said yes.
You didn't want to be cruel.

You smelled just like flowers.
I should've cheered.
I could've sniffed you for hours.
Wait. Is that weird? Don't be weird!
Be brave and EMPOWER!!

Your voice was as sweet as a melody.
Your eyes make me want to set my heart free.

In this chaos and confusion hereof,
you came down from the heavens up above.
Is this love? This is love. I am in love!!

## *February 14: Two Hearts, One Love*

We drift upon blankets of fluffy clouds,
far above chaos of this modern star.
I gaze in your galaxy eyes, proudly.
How can this dream last always, where we are?

The heavens created this seat for you.
Creation grows ever replete for you.
The drum of my heart ever beats for you.
My soul's song became complete just for you…

I confess my feels from every mountain.
I'd compress time just to stay here, it's true.
Our pleasant wonderland is for certain.
My present and future belong with you…

For as long as you vibe the way I do,
I will stay here where this true love ensues.

### *February 27: Vulnerably Shy*

Not so long ago, there was a boy, Shy.
A boy who saw the world so differently.
Where others could only see black and white,
Shy felt every color, his favorite green…

As Shy lived his world of beautiful hues,
others shunned him, threw rocks, and called him names.
No love was shown by those who're supposed to.
Even his parents could only feel shame…

At ten and two, a man showed him olde ways.
As his natural beauty was undone,
his colors were bleached, and he learned the blade,
leaving him to see but shades of crimson…

His heart turned soot black, and lungs filled with smoke,
as he lost all sense of beauty and hope.

## *March 1: A Fool for You*

I'm caught in your gravity more and more,
each and every day that goes by when I'm

Basking in your light,
watching your mind bright
find new ways to write
"I love you" just right

Across the stitches of my open scars
as master of this human condition.

Sans the need to think,
my soul is your ink.
My heart, yours to prink,
wrapped 'round your pinky.

And I could get lost in the swirls and curls
of your colorful imagination.

Like petals in the wind—
love treasures destined
for each me to find
his way through the grind—

Each kiss is an ethereal moment
to be held tight, and forever cherished.

## *March 16: Angel*

With supple fingers running through my hair,
you caress emotions with your soft touch.
With ease, you radiate warmth everywhere.
How can one person give so very much?

Your amour's an angelic breath in Spring,
bringing divine life to each weary soul,
easing the lonely pain and suffering,
mending the broken and making them whole…

The smile in your eyes fills my withered veins.
The kiss from your lips thrills my beating heart.
The wealth of your love still can't be explained.
I hope with each fiber we never part.

If you ever left, my whole world would end,
so, I'll be thankful for the time we spend.

### *March 19: Moon-Blessed*

Undressed

Silver rays rest,

Perfectly perched upon

Your crown of silky goddess hair,

Wise laurels, tied in buns.

My head to breast.

Moon-blessed.

## *April 2: Fate's Design*

In the majesty of your golden eyes
sparkles the warm light of one thousand stars.
In a grand world of gargantuan size,
how did I come to be right where you are?

Like the desert palm upon sandy shore,
bending and breaking against the cold wind,
love and loss have shattered me to the core.
But with your love grows new hope from within.

Of every stone brought in by the swole tide,
I thank the Universe that you chose mine.
You bubble with giggles from a smile wide,
(and perhaps a small amount of red wine),

But you shine fate's monumental design.
And I'm proud, and grateful, to call you mine.

## *April 4: Fifteen Things I Love About You*

I love your magnetic charm.
How you can command a room,
simply by announcing your name…

I love the tattoos on your arm.
How you can take doom and gloom,
And send them back where they came…

I love your honey and spice,
And everything in between.
Like a hot chai on a winter's day…

I love how you think I'm a prize,
when really, I've nothing been
but over-complicated…

I love your naughty and wild side.
How you take me for a ride, and
leave me never wanting to let go…

I love the shine in your smile.
In your eyes, for a long while,
 lies a future waiting to grow.

You excite me.
You invite me.
You incite me.
You delight me
when you skite of me,
and limelight me…

But so much more importantly,
I love the way you make my heart
daydream away the long day…

…in the way you are, naturally.
A light chasing away the dark.
And I love how neither of us would have it any other way.

## *April 13: Love, Infinitely*

Whisper into my ear,

as soft and gently as a summer's breeze,

how you need me as I need you…

How your heart SHOUTS what ears can't hear,

with pure, unfettered ease,

the things you'll always hold true…

Proclaim, with jubilant cheer,

from the heights of the Pyrenees,

to the depths of our oceans blue…

Tell how you've waited ten thousand years,

for one as caring as me,

to finally speak, "I do" …

Say you'll be my forever, Dear…

and I'll say, in perpetuity,

I will love you, infinitely, too.

## *April 28: Vow (Dearly Beloved)*

Dearly Beloved, we gather here today
'cause I have something important to say
to the one I'll always call my Bae-Bae.

We have been through so much over last year,
from living it up to coping with fear.
But I wouldn't trade a day, so three cheers!

As you stand before me right here, right now,
e'en now, I have trouble believing how
you'd love someone like me, and this I vow:

To love you more than myself.
To n'er put you on the shelf.
To keep you close to my heart.
Always hate being apart.
To be there through thick and thin.
Always see beauty within.
For eternity, from now.

This, I vow.

## *May 1: Blossom in the Rain*

Sweetly you slumber, dreaming of candy-coated clouds.
Gentle rain drips to the beating of your pristine heart.
Ne'er in my unimpressive life have I felt more proud
to protect our blossoming love til death does us part...

Our two imperfect halves form an immaculate whole,
illuminating the darkness of vacuous space.
So beautifully delicate, like a newborn soul.
So vulnerable, yet resilient and unafraid...

Warmth from our love radiates like destiny achieved,
pulsing through the midnight sky across the lonely sea.
Ne'er in my misfortunate life would I have believed
that one as heavenly perfect as you would choose me.

This moment frozen in time— may I ne'er let you go.

## *May 8: The Feels*

I love the way the morning light
falls gently
upon your intoxicating smile.
Your silky hair flows on for miles,
like fields of strawberry kisses bathing in the sun…

I love the way you move,
swaying side to side
to the beats of your own drum.
Stylishly hip, and then some.
Rhythmically mesmerizing…

I love the compassion in your eyes,
understanding,
as if you've lived one thousand lives,
rooting for the underdog every time.
Saintly endearing.

I love the way you make me feel.
Naturally high,

floating on a cloud through a dream.

Even better than it could ever seem.

In peace.

## *May 19: Always You*

The morning star rises in the blue sky,
as twitter-birds begin to sing their song.
The misty mountain fog clears, like my mind,
as my way to you reveals, before long.

All my life, I've looked for someone to love,
searching from rocky shore to shining sea.
I've turned every stone, below and above,
yet all along, you were in front of me.

And as I get lost in your soulful eyes,
hearing from your heart more than words can say,
no more do I need to find reasons why
I have had to watch as love ran away.

For, it's you who has always held the key,
to mend the pieces of this secret me.

## *May 24: Just Once*

There you are upon the wall,
gazing down upon it all.
Wonder what it would be like…
Should be like riding a bike.
Just once.

I saved you for just a day
like this crazy day today.
Maybe just a baby blaze…
Stop looking at me that way.
Just once!

As I load up the glass pipe,
the vibe begins to feel ripe.
Who the hell needs to be proud?
It feels good blowing some cloud.
Just once.

Lord, hasn't it been a while
since anything made me smile…

…and this high won't even drop!

But now I think I can't stop…

Just once.

## *May 28: Old Habits*

Hot. Sweat. Burn. Breathe.
Jump. Slide. Pow. Reef.
Hit it. Don't quit it.

Light it. Nine clouds.
Don't fight it. Shout!
In… and out… shit!

Coughing and dropping.
Laughing like taffy.
Glass all on the floor.

Knocking and rocking.
Stashing and cashing
in, through the back door.

Tank it. Crank it.
Dank it. Bank it.
No net by the wall.

Fake it. Take it.
Shake it. Bake it.
Shots at last call…

Fading… in the bathroom stall.

## *June 2: Breezy and Young*

Bae… we've had some heavy conversations.
Why not give in to some relaxation?
We could escape all the automation.
We could run away to our paradise…

I remember those perfect moments when
the sun would come out to warm the cold air,
kissing away all our doubts and nonsense,
and led to pristine beaches without care…

Bae… remember those days when we were young?
We both got heart tattoos, you pierced your tongue,
and no upbeat melody went unsung?
We snuck into clubs, dancing 'til sunrise…

Happily, evocative beats would play
along the coast and up into the hills.
We'd let down our hair and dance by the bay,
stomping charmed feet to melodious thrills…

What I would give to go back to those times!
Those were the days of our enchanted prime…

My Bae… long before the struggles and strife,
we were so drunk on love in blissful life.
That was when I asked you to be my wife.
How your beautiful eyes still mesmerize!

We were so touched by serendipity,
two-stepping to every tune we heard,
completely immune to the unhappy.
We lived every cheerful, joyful word…

So, before we go back to rainy skies,
kiss me once more, in our youthful reprise.

## *June 10: La Vie en Rose*

We slowly dance beneath the dream-light tree.
Upon your wrist, you wear my beating heart.
In your starry eyes, you hold all of me.
Yet still, I fear the day that we must part…

Like a brilliant new, diamond moon you shine
against the midnight sky of my dark soul.
Why a goddess so pristine and divine
would choose scum like me, I will never know…

I dread the day you wake and realize
perfect angels like you can't love demons.
Where you bring hopeful devotion and light,
my fears and doubts are worthy of no one.

But until that day, I will hold you close,
dreaming of our life together in rose."

## *July 4: A Mistake*

You say to look you in the eyes.
You say to tell you the truth.
So, I do, I don't even lie,
but you continue to accuse!

I said I would try to quit,
but I can't make no promises.
You think I make too light of it.
I think you are too dismissive.

You knew what you're getting into.
Never said I was some pure saint.
If you want a prize you can fix too,
open those cold eyes, 'cause I ain't!

It's supposed to be give and take.
Maybe this was a big mistake…

## *July 7: Here and Forever*

People always ask me where you are and
how I can still be in love with a ghost.
But my baby, they just don't understand.
Is it wrong to love you the very most?

When I saw you descend heaven's great stairs,
I knew then that you must be an angel
come to answer each one of my prayers,
come to rescue me from that lonely hell.

The way you glow brightens every room.
The way you smile always heightens my mood.
The way you show how to blossom and bloom
strums the strings of my heart beating for you.

Though you may come like Spring after Winter,
I'll keep loving you. Here, and forever.

## *July 14: Sunset Nigh*

My
Darkness
Will descend
Mightily so
But for now, I must
Hold tightly to
Light you've sent
Sunset
Nigh

## *August 1: Harsh*

Your harsh words pierce like chalkboard's cries.
What do you know of life's freedoms?
It brings but hunger and pained lies,
leaving us hatefully spurned, numb.
There's no room for us hopeless scum.

What ever happened to true love,
the kind that sees beyond our sins?
What I could use from up above,
a mind that freely grows within
a sign that we meet halfway in.

You say I am wasting away,
that I squander gifts I'm given.
I say just walk the other way
if you can't bear what I've hidden.
Goodbye. Au revoir. Good riddance.

Leaving, no?
Fine. Just go.

## *August 24: Wretch*

As we walk beneath the stars' light,
and the pale moon lends us a smile,
I want to make everything right,
to bask in your warmth for a while…

But as the cold night stretches on,
so, too, does the dark of my soul.
Though I dream for the break of dawn,
she's forever beyond my hold…

For I'm just a wretch without hope,
whose only home lay amongst blades
covered in lonely gin and dope,
digging the bones until they break…

Better to run the other way,
before you burn in the black blaze.

# LOSS

## *September 11: How?*

Sirens. Phone calls. Can't hear at all.
Earthquake. Landslide. Just want to hide.
How could this be?

Music. Playing. PD saying.
Loud drums. Crashing. 'Tatoes mashing.
How could this be?

Driving. Writhing. Irving. First Spring.
Paving. Caving. Racing. Saving.
How could this…?

Lying. Sighing. Crying. Dying.
Dread head sped, led Fred said, bled, spread.
How could…?

Dead.

How?

## *September 19: Beloved*

Dearly Beloved, we gather here today,
in this very sudden and tragic way,
in order to say what we couldn't say,
in life.

Dearly Beloved, let us celebrate
our memories rather than contemplate
all the details that led to this sad fate,
and strife.

Our Beloved Friends from every end,
we must try to bend, try to heal and mend,
so we can ascend, and not dwell or spend…
…but why?

She was ripped from my arms in dead of night.
Given to me, like, just kidding, boy! Sike!
So, why should we all look to the bright sight?!
Take a hike.

Beloved.

## *September 23: Ash in the Wind*

Rain from a black sky falls upon my face,
cascading like tears, were they left to cry.
Empty and numb, I stare off into space,
unbelieving of reality's lie…

Pelted by sands of ephemeral time
slipping through my trembling hands' tightened grip,
her last light ebbs and fades above the rime.
My mind begins to stall, wither and skip.

For how could a rose of unmatched beauty,
borne on wings of the sparkling, diamond moon,
crumble like ash in the winds of the sea?
A crimson-eyed loon wails his mournful tune…

Like a lapdog bereft of his master,
I stare in silence on muddy pasture,
waiting for she who'll never come again…

## *October 12: Empty and Alone*

Just who do you think you are,
sitting upon our golden clouds?
Who made you God, to leave ajar,
from afar, my bleeding heart,
stripping all the love I'm allowed?

How could you just up and leave,
without taking me with you?
Why wear my love on your sleeve,
just to cleave all we conceived,
as I choke in the cold blue?

Why are you incredibly weak?
How could you let go of her shine?
You found the real thing, but chose tweak
every week, instead of seeking
to say one-four-three one more time…

Now you're alone,
in empty home,

where nothing's grown.

## *October 31: 'F' is for Fear*

A black fog quietly invades,
slowly tightening its apt grip.
The scent of doom blossoms pervades,
suffocating both throat and lips.
'Sundering soul it tears and rips.

Sinking, shriveling eyes go black.
'Pon brow, a failing mark embossed,
a reminder of all that lacks,
every opportune moment lost,
each daring dream shredded and tossed.

The drumming of blood behind ears
overwhelms the sounds of my screams.
As I begin to drown in tears,
reality unbinds the seams,
fracturing every support beam.

How can this be?
Who will save me?

## *November 11: Now that You're Gone*

I miss your clothes everywhere on the floor,
even though it would make me so crazy.
I miss the decorations on the door,
e'en the frog you thought was so amazing.

I miss the perpetual lilac scent,
even on the bottom of every shoe.
Miss that spot on the back of your knee's bend,
'cause each little bit was a part of you…

Your favorite orchids lie withered and dry.
The jigsaw lies scattered and pulled apart.
No tears even remain, for me to cry,
like the silence of my once beating heart.

No more will I wake to your smile at dawn,
now that you're gone…

## *December 7: Snowflake*

The frigid wind blew and blew.

And with it, suffering.

Mother took pity,

sending her love,

bringing here

to me,

you.

Lovely,

without fear,

falling above

my snowflake beauty.

Though you'll melt, come the Spring,

I'll always be loving you.

## *December 31: Panic*

Help.

Get me out of this place.

I can't stop bawling.

Eyes are flaring,

and I'm shaking at my base.

My skin is crawling, and everyone is staring at my face.

Please help.

My chest labors and heaves.

I wish you were here.

The low walls are closing,

and I can't breathe.

I miss when you're near 'cause you know how to show
       me how to leave.

Help me.

What would you do?

You would tell me to chill,

Take me to the cold,

Tell them I have the flu.

Say you had your fill, cross the threshold, and play the
>ingénue.

Calm.

Breathe.

Just be.

## *January 2: Loveless*

The doors so firmly stick.
I lie as wounded foal.
Have I become so sick?
Sick in both chest and soul?

I cannot even breathe,
as my mind turns to fears.
Lungs empty, yet replete.
Replete with ceaseless tears.

The night you walked away,
my knees buckled, I swayed.
Couldn't sing, couldn't play.
Dissonance rules my daze.

Your warm love was my cure.
But now, I die, for sure.

A stark chill fills the air.
The wind rattles my bones.

Panic turns to despair.
Will you ever come home?
Our love was like lightning,
dancing from cloud to cloud.
Passionately crashing.
Thunderingly proud.

Now days wither and fade,
crumbling like dreamless jade.
Each prized moment unmade,
like pawns we never played.

Your heart was gentle, pure.
Loveless, I die. For sure.

## *January 11: Illing*

More storm clouds linger here on the home front,
though I sweat when I should really shiver.
In my sleep, I mumble, I stumble, grunt.
Please, some chronic, not tonics, cod liver.

As I lie motionless in the cold snow,
my vacant head pounds with silent disgust.
Wish I could just hold you and not let go,
but I'm not worthy of your pristine trust.

My place belongs with the dying and dead.
Saints like you deserve angels up on high,
immaculately dressed in golden threads,
not dumb bums like me, who can't get it right.

I can't be anything more than a fluke,
choking on his own toxic soot and puke.

## *February 2: Alone*

A winter breeze roams the halls.
Stagnant, with no place to go.
Your laughter once echoed off the walls.
But now, there's a still silence so
thick that nothing can even grow…

I miss all of the little things.
The pitter-patter of footsteps.
The joy your morning tea would bring.
Ways your words across my heart swept.
But I just can't seem to accept…

You're gone.

Without any reason or rhyme,
how can I live in worlds so blue?
To move forward, I keep trying.
But only one thing e'er seems true.
I just cannot live without you.

Who will help me conquer my fears?
Who will smile with those twinkling eyes?
Who will wipe away all the tears?
With whom will I share each sunrise?
Unending night grows cold, and I'm…

Alone.

## *February 13: The Lake*

Aimless, I wander the lake's shore,
lost, like this hidden gem we knew.
Thought I might find answers, or more,
but I'm only left missing you…

The sun no longer warms and shines.
No rainbowed gold blesses with luck.
Where once we heard whispers divine,
now lie vast fields of mud and muck.

Carefree clouds drift, heavy with rain,
as thunder rolls in the distance.
Photo memories just bring pain,
for never again shall we dance.

The Old Oak just reminds you're gone,
and I'm without home, all alone.

## *February 23: Lovenado*

We were a funnel cloud,
swirling and storming
through the onyx sky.
No warning.
No mercy.
Destroying everything in our path,
each kiss
passionately striking the ground
with enamored thunderbolts,
until suddenly…
you were gone.

### *March 15: Okay?*

Funny we got caught going the same way.
Look like I got hit by a train, he says?
Am I okay?

He says I look as pale as a moon ray.
Do I need a hotel or place to stay?
Am I okay?

Well, I could use some cloud to take away
all of the illing from this kinda cray…
…okay?

Nay?

Then, why the fuck did a turncoat schmuck,
in his beat-up truck, ask about my luck,
okay?

Should really just end calling him a friend.
Go back where he went? Can piss off, get bent!

I couldn't pay my rent.

Okay?!

## *March 31: The Nightmare*

The long shadows of everlasting night
tear away at the moon's pale, gentle light.
A deep darkness taints what was true and right.
Heat from soot and smoke is my only friend…

As the shades and demons come out to play,
clouds of regret stifle what I can say,
suffocating my lungs with ashen gray.
I wait for the inevitable end…

With gnashing teeth and thrashing claws, they feed
upon the empty husk that once was me.
Bones crack like thunder over the black sea
until at last there's nothing left to rend…

A faceless figure with a crooked smile
strikes wicked chords, dissonant, maligned, vile
from its tower of tortured souls a while,
until time no longer exists to spend.

What hero yet lives in pure, holy light,

to save me from this endless, hopeless plight?

## *April 2: The Slums*

Here in the underworld shadows,
where even angel tears don't reach,
I look through these broken windows
with nobody left to beseech…

Painted clouds cry blood on the walls,
as melted spoon drips toxic dreams.
It seems like forever since Fall,
Yet I still waste in crimson streams…

Sometimes I still catch a glimpse fair
of our turbulent life in rain,
but when I see you looking there,
I know only regret and shame…

All I can do is turn away.
It's best to close my eyes and sleep,
since nothing yet remains to say.
There's no hope for demons like me…

Love's a game I don't want to play.

We losers just can never win.

Winners never turn out okay,

and no one leaves scot-free of sin…

As your words echo in my head,

I wonder if it's over yet…

## *April 4: Venice Beach*

The sun softly sets over Venice Beach.
The festive day starts to come to a close,
yet again, you remain beyond my reach,
where skies full of memories cooled and froze…

Drifting upon a wave from the doldrums,
a lone, melancholy Spanish guitar,
pricking with poignantly accurate strums,
chords of my perpetually bleeding heart…

How could the brilliance of our diamond star
flicker, fracture and fade into the rift?
The more I search for signs of you afar,
the more I realize how much you're missed…

As the cold darkness fills my empty eyes,
I hope you wish for me, too, 'pon same skies…

## *April 12: Incomplete*

It's three a.m.
Nothing stirs.
Silenced, like the melody of my soul...

The sky's still black.
Air is so cold.
Stillborn, just like the rhythm of my heart...

You were so kind.
Always giving.
And here I can't even give to myself...

What do I do?
Where do I go?
How can I live without hearing your voice?

I made my bed.
Now I must lie.
I get the feeling the best I can be...

Is incomplete…

Wish it had been me.

## *April 17: The Monster Beneath My Veins*

Like diamonds, your soul radiantly shines
with the brilliance of one thousand new stars.
Your presence illuminates every line,
reminding why I can't be where you are…

You glide with unbreakably refined grace.
Your magic moon waxes, my spirit wanes.
You showcase the best in the human race.
I recall my efforts being in vain…

In your naturally perfected world,
I'm the blemishes of deep-rooted scars.
The black hatred and shame within me swirl.
The light in my soul remains purely scarce…

I want only sever the binding chains
to release the monster beneath my veins.

## *May 1: Frozen in Crimson*

The whole world froze
the night you went away.
Freedom you chose.
I didn't have a say,
and while you doze
happily by the bay,
I just feel lows.
Too gone to be okay.

For me, time's still,
stuck remembering when
I got real ill.
Felt like I had the bends,
but you stayed 'til
we were more than just friends.
By window's sill,
we hugged like two bookends…

But now I bleed, lying in the bathtub,
cold and all alone, bereft of your love.

Dying and afraid, like some wounded cub,
my heart gutted, stopped on the crimson rug.

# REBIRTH

## *May 29: Hi, and Hello (Part 2)*

Hi, Doc…and hello.
I probably seem messed up, but
I used to be pretty mellow…
I smoke cloud, and… I tend to cut.
And I can't get out of this rut…

They bust down the door. I was dead,
lost somewhere amongst all the stars,
in a bathtub covered in red.
But a good friend in The Great War
was quick to bring me where we are…

I've been under the blade for years…
Began again, we lost the grins
when I couldn't control the fear.
Guilt from unforgivable sins.
I should have been looking within…

I drowned in black, the hatred whorled.
Before long, she too lost her way.

We abandoned our entire world.

Neither could ever be the same…

I do not know what else to say.

## *June 14: Lacrimae Lunae (Tears of the Moon)*

Great doom has descended.
Creation is ended.
Fire ravishes the land.
Man turns against Woman.
Seven seas rage and swell.
Heavens fill with soot fell.
Crops turn putrid, rotten.
The gods are forgotten…

But know, you are not alone,
for hope is not all yet gone.
Each day still, the sun will rise.
and at night, the Great Wolf cries
to the moon's pure, holy light,
that Man be saved from his plight.
The White Dove will end all wars,
bathed in the light of the stars.

Earth, wind, sea and fire will calm,
by the Phoenix's soothing balm.

Man shall remember he's loved,
From afar, from above.

*June 21: Thunder*

Thunder rolls across open plains.

I mope beneath the falling rain

of a seemingly ceaseless storm…


Near a year has come and gone

since I last knew the coming dawn.

Despair somehow became the norm…


Yet, I find comfort in this place,

and as the rain kisses my face,

I recall the warmth we once shared…


Times of endless sun and skies blue,

But turbulent winds, dark clouds, too.

Still, we loved like no one else dared…

Behind each storm's a golden sun

waiting for darkness to be done,

drying the stoop of every door…


And if the sun must rise each day,

to send all the black rain away,

then I want to be sad no more.


I will rise, and climb once again,

above these thunderous plains' pain,

to remember what we live for.

## *July 3: Oath of the Brave*

The darkness reigns this unending midnight.
No star's light can save you from the grim's doom.
Your friends have yielded to unholy light.
Why resist the might of the crushing gloom?

Sleep now, child, for your savior is long spent.
Your sword has dulled, and your shield is broken.
You have squandered the boons your gods have lent.
Forgotten prayers your saints had once spoken.

Let the cold of the tides snuff futile flames.
Let your soul be swept by encroaching black.
For it has lost the way from whence it came,
and the winds of change have stilled at your back.

Eternal rest awaits, child of Adam.
You need but kneel before all that I am.

Darkness of unyielding night rains, indeed.
The pale moon's might has long since waxed and waned.
The black shroud I could wear too easily.
Would not my brothers' courage be in vain?

From the deepest depths, I proclaim, "nay."
So that none more may see your wicked blight.
'Til my blood has boiled and withered away,
may the sun's light shine once more. I will fight!

Taking up the mantles of fallen friends,
whose names I etch on memory's keen edge,
whose honor I will forever defend,
I will smite you where you lie. This, I pledge!

Die, demon of loneliness and despair,
'pon Lightbringer, my unwavering prayer!

## *July 4: Stars in the Night*

Watchful eyes burst into tears,
as war-torn fields erupt with screams.
Shards shrill and pierce from broken mirrors,
cutting through the pungent smokescreens…

Since the birth of the new dawn,
blind hatred for the unknown has
beaten, broken, stood upon us
like unwanted property owned.

Bones may splinter and shatter.
Bullets may cause us to scatter.
The same, our mortal husks splatter.
But deep in our defiant eyes
burns the wills of the victimized.
Though crushed by the vehement lies,

We rise.

With bold stripes of glaring tails,

our rockets soar through evening skies,
exploding with ten million hails,
in every color and size.

While watchful eyes burst into tears
of liberated joy and pride,
our war-torn fields erupt with cheers,
persisting like stars in the night.

## *July 13: Dirge for Our Ephemeral Youth*

There was a time, long ago, I recall,
when there were never regrets or mistakes—
long before the need to build all the walls.
Heads never bowed and backs would never break,
as we were the masters of our own fates…

With a wave of our imaginations,
and armed with no more than a ballpoint pen,
we could weave the grandest of vacations—
atop the highest peaks, in dragons' dens,
under the vast seas, or in Willow's Glen…

But once all of the stories had been told,
the harsh and real overtook, dusk and dawn.
Our world became irreversibly cold.
Time came to settle reckless abandon,
so we paid our growing tab, and moved on…

Chance would rule; our magic slowly faded,
for every child grows old, worn and jaded.

Carlin W. Allen / Letters from a Lost Soul

## *July 26: SS-42*

How radiantly does the single star
glow before the shine of two thousand suns?
More so for the passing gaze from afar,
unaware of the triumphs of the one?

Though she passionately burns with all might,
traversing through chaotic galaxies,
what use is even most resplendent light,
when drowned by visual cacophonies?

Overwhelmed by greatness beyond her skill,
she silently slips into deep despair,
to feel the vacuous darkness's chill,
believing not a soul remains who cares…

Fret not, for Mother Universe still loves,
and would mourn even one lost ray hereof.

## *July 31: In Mirrors*

When I look in mirrors, what do I see
beneath the various layers of me?
Am I strikingly handsome? Am I tall?
And am I worthy to hang on this wall?

When I look upon this sick, pallid face,
I see cracks with painted masks in their place.
Long, fissured scars, running deeply and wide.
Places where a hurt little boy does hide...

Through deeds of those he was to trust the most,
he learned even love has a heavy cost.
He wandered in the dark, broken and lost,
succumbing to the hatred in the frost.

Until one day, he found a pale moonbeam.
She glowed and sparkled in a silver stream.
For what must have been fifteen thousand dreams,
he cherished her with the highest esteem.

In each twinkle of her silvery glow,
a love, one for the other, swelled and flowed.
But one night, Mother Moon called her back home.
Again, in the dark, the boy was alone…

You ask what lies in mirrors on the wall.
I see a tortured boy in hoarfrost squall,
much too afraid to love, with wounded heart.
Those who dare to love are destined to part.

## *August 11: Starlight*

As I lie beneath a blanket of stars,
watching the world turn without you and I,
I wish I could be wherever you are,
somewhere we'd never have to say goodbye…

In truth, don't know how to live missing you.
Your stars are the only ones I pray to.
Your ears are the only ones I sing to.
Your heart's the only place my love stays…

Though I hope we still wish on the same sky,
for you, I know I must try to be brave,
hoping some day we rejoin, you and I,
so I can give you as much as you gave.

Until then, I'll remember your bright smile,
healing beneath your starlight for a while.

## *August 16: Happy Birthday*

This year has come and gone.
The seasons of my soul once more change.
Anger and disbelief first reigned,
then my last words plagued me with guilt.
But as I sit alone with stones,

I wish you were near,
I wish you were here
to quiet my fear,
whisper in my ear,
say our future's clear,
and I will wear you
around my breaking heart…

I know we lie beneath same skies,
and someday I'll hold you again.
Though it continues to rain,
I remember the way you filled
me with your love, deep in my bones—

The fire in your eyes,
burning far too bright
to e'er fade and die,
warmed sorrowful cries
from my changing tides
with heart that don't hide.
Though we said goodbye,

I need just look at our brilliant star,
high above the Lonely Mountains,
to know nothing has really changed.
Armed with our love at the hilt,
what we have can ne'er be undone…

I will be brave, as
devoutly I say,

Happy Birthday

## *August 20: Renaissance*

Dear Mom and Dad,

Sorry I couldn't be the perfect son.

I guess that I was born shattered and sad.

I wish that I had been born to no one.

Dear Dad and Mom,

Wish that I had been worthy of your love,

Rather than being disappointment bombs.

But why'd you have to break me from above?

A "special" kind of punishment you'd give,

and now I remember everything.

The slaps, the shoves, the kicks, ten broken ribs,

and all the bloodied scars your "love" would bring.

And now that I know the source of my blues,

sorry, but I have to cut you (off) too.

## *August 23: Threads and Bubbles*

Carried by golden threads

floating high above at midnight,

memories

shimmer and glow,

each one

an effervescent bubble in time.

Soft to the touch.

Warm to the hearth.

Loving windows

peering deep into the souls

of two serendipitous fools,

torn apart by life's cruelties…

Still…

Like crumbs in a timeworn fairytale,

each thread

leads me back

to you.

*September 2: Fireside*

I've always lived like a flame in the wind,
stretching skyward, trying to match your light,
to inspire, reach higher, from within,
but you are always just beyond my sight…

In this cold, lonely night, it's hard to see
which path to follow, which way to turn.
When I climb to the top of every tree,
each one that I touch just withers and burns…

How can I want me the way you loved me?
Haunt with that infectious smile above me…

Stay and baffle me.
Be riffraff with me.
Laugh the way you'd say
you'd never let go…

Lie and tickle me,

your love trickling

'til we're sick and we

fly in through life's flow…

I won't sit idly while life passes by.

I will continue to reach t'ward the sky,

fighting each night, 'til my light finds your eyes,

holding you the way I always meant to,

Fireside.

## *September 16: Tetra Station*

I woke up at Tetra Station.
No idea how I got there…
Played out like some animation.
But you were there, brushing your hair…

I saw you and began to cry.
You looked over and simply smiled.
It was enough, I don't know why,
to see you happy for a while.

Wanted to stay and watch us grow,
but I heard a strange sort of chime
telling me I needed to go,
because it wasn't yet my time.

I turned to ask for one request,
just as our show faded to white.
Wanted to feel us at our best…
…just to know we would be alright.

Just to forget all of the rest…

## *September 19: Lovesworn*

Once upon a cold, lonely winter's day,
you graced me with the brilliance of your soul.
For a moment, our love burned, come what may,
but foolishly I threw it upon shoals…

Only now that The Great Divide's between
do I realize how precious you were.
There isn't a road I have not been,
searching for something so beautifully sure—

Hope amongst despair.
Diamond of drake lair.
Luminously clear.
Yet I feigned I didn't care…

If only I'd stayed,
and not have betrayed
the vows that we made,
I'd be holding you this day…

So, I will live out the rest of my life,
not wasting a single second of time
poisoning this gift you've given to me,
and from whatever heaven you will see—

I will spend ten thousand lonely lifetimes,
I'll cross ten thousand ethereal blues,
rummaging through the most bitter of climes
to find e'en the smallest chance back to you…

Back to the pristine love that we once knew.

## *September 21: I See You*

I see you
in bright clouds billowy,
floating high up above
on a mild summer breeze…

I see you
in each melodious refrain,
as we conspicuously dance
to the beats of the rain…

I see you on vacuous nights,
twinkling pristinely,
keeping diligent watch
over we who dream…

I see you in the eyes of children,
awestruck and amazed,
at each slight of hand
life gives away…

In whispers of the wind,
And shadows of the sun,
I see you.

On untrodden trails
of enchanting evening runs,
I see you.

From bubbly daydreams
and nighttime slumbers,
I see you.

To wailing willows,
deep in the thunder,
I see you.

In every thought and step and hum and morning rise,
in every smile and wink and laugh and soothing sigh,
in the gentle glowing of my heart,

I will <u>always</u>

Keep you.

## *September 30: Cloud Bubbles*

"Wake up. Wake up, sleepyhead.
You'll miss the rising of the sun.
Come watch colors change," you said,
"The long and cold night is now done.

"Open up your eyes and see,
the heavens put on shows for you."
You were beaming bright at me.
I had forgotten all my blues.

We lay on blankets of clouds,
blowing bubbles into the wind.
Yours were biggest. You were proud.
Warmth without became warmth within.

As the pink turned to orange,
I wanted to stay there a while…
It felt familiar, yet strange,
just there wanting to watch you smile…

Hugging and loving me.

On our clouds over the sea.

## *October 3: Happiest*

Sleepily I open my eyes.
You sweetly smile down at me.
The sun slowly begins to rise
over our home above the sea,
and there's nowhere I'd rather be…

Through great fields of giant tulips,
we hide, and run, and laugh, and play.
You spin me around on your hips.
We joyfully enjoy the day,
and there's nowhere I'd rather stay…

When the moonlight shines down on us,
and the stars come out to say
the time has come in which we must
bid goodnight and part separate ways,
and there's nowhere else I'd rather lay,

Than in your arms, this boy of "thray,"
this happiest of Mother's Days.

## *October 10: Fern*

I drift upon an endless sea of black.
Cold, empty, and unyielding, as inside.
Vacuously beyond sense and reason…

Where once flew swarms of stars, from front to back,
like fairy-dusted fireflies in night skies,
stagnates darkness which snuffed each last beacon…

As I stare at the vacancy above,
in the distance I hear her melody—
soft, and delicate, like butterfly wings.

She leads me to a time of joy… and love.
Uneventful, but completely carefree.
Just her. Just me. Listening to her sing.

Underneath a brilliant diamond ocean,
it was she who captivated my heart,
the night she agreed to become my wife…

Icy tears fall, birthing one million suns.

In this moment, I know we'll never part,

and once again, spores of light spring to life.

So long as candles of memory burn,

she is with me, eternally— my Fern.

## *October 17: Awakening*

I
awoke
finally
for the first time
with peace in my heart,
hearing wind chimes,
feeling free,
not broke.
Chi.

## *November 6: "Home"*

Sweetly the morning birds sing,
announcing the newborn day,
as the dawn stretches her rays,
giving warmth and offering
clear heavens in which to play…

Cheerfully the river flows
from atop the snow-capped peaks.
White willows hear the wind speak,
as salmon swim to and fro,
and Great Grandfather Owl sleeps…

A gentle breeze bears soft hymns
across cliffs where ibex roam.
Below, falls bubble and foam,
filling twin lakes to the brim.
In this place where I call home.

## *November 27: I See You*

I see you

in bright clouds billowy,

floating high up above

on a mild summer breeze…


I see you

in each melodious refrain,

as we conspicuously dance

to the beats of the rain…


I see you on vacuous nights,

twinkling pristinely,

keeping diligent watch

over we who dream…


I see you in the eyes of children,

awestruck and amazed,

at each slight of hand

life gives away…


In whispers of the wind,

And shadows of the sun,

I see you.


On untrodden trails

of enchanting evening runs,

I see you.


From bubbly daydreams

and nighttime slumbers,

I see you.


To wailing willows,

deep in the thunder,

I see you.

In every thought and step and hum and morning rise,

in every smile and wink and laugh and soothing sigh,

in the gentle glowing of my heart,

I will *always*

Keep you.

## "CHOCTAW PRAYER"

"The track of the sun across the sky leaves its shining, eternal message, illuminating, strengthening, and warming all of us who are here. It shows us we are not alone."

## **Acknowledgements**

Special thanks to all the people who inspired, encouraged, promoted and believed in me, including but not limited to my husband, my friends, family, my second-year college English teacher, and of course, you the readers. Without all of you, I may never have put words to paper.

So, thank you. From the bottom of my heart.

## **Social Media**

Instagram: @cwapoetry

Threads: @cwapoetry

To request permissions, please email:

cwapoetry@pm.me

www.ingramcontent.com/pod-product-compliance
Lightning Source LLC
LaVergne TN
LVHW092051060526
838201LV00047B/1337